ABOUT THE BANK STREET READY-TO-READ SERIES

More than seventy-five years of educational research, innovative teaching, and quality publishing have earned The Bank Street College of Education its reputation as America's most trusted name in early childhood education.

Because no two children are exactly alike in their development, the Bank Street Ready-to-Read series is written on three levels to accommodate the individual stages of reading readiness of children ages three through eight.

○ *Level 1:* GETTING READY TO READ **(Pre-K–Grade 1)**
Level 1 books are perfect for reading aloud with children who are getting ready to read or just starting to read words or phrases. These books feature large type, repetition, and simple sentences.

● *Level 2:* READING TOGETHER **(Grades 1–3)**
These books have slightly smaller type and longer sentences. They are ideal for children beginning to read by themselves who may need help.

○ *Level 3:* I CAN READ IT MYSELF **(Grades 2–3)**
These stories are just right for children who can read independently. They offer more complex and challenging stories and sentences.

All three levels of The Bank Street Ready-to-Read books make it easy to select the books most appropriate for your child's development and enable him or her to grow with the series step by step. The levels purposely overlap to reinforce skills and further encourage reading.

We feel that making reading fun is the single most important thing anyone can do to help children become good readers. We hope you will become part of Bank Street's long tradition of learning through sharing.

The Bank Street College of Education

Jim — This one's for you
— E.L.S.

To my sisters,
Alexis and Penelope
— L.C.K.

ᴍ ω

For a free color catalog describing Gareth Stevens' list of high-quality books and multimedia programs, call 1-800-542-2595 (USA) or 1-800-461-9120 (Canada). Gareth Stevens Publishing's Fax: (414) 225-0377.
See our catalog, too, on the World Wide Web: http://gsinc.com

Library of Congress Cataloging-in-Publication Data

Schecter, Ellen.
    The warrior maiden : a Hopi legend / by Ellen Schecter; illustrated by Laura Kelly.
        p.   cm. -- (Bank Street ready-to-read)
    Originally published: New York: Bantam Books, © 1992.
        Summary: A retelling of the Indian legend in which Huh-áy-ay, a brave Hopi girl, helps to save her peaceful pueblo from Apache raiders.
        ISBN 0-8368-1696-X (lib. bdg.)
        1. Hopi Indians--Folklore.   2. Folklore--Arizona.   [1. Hopi Indians--Folklore.   2. Indians of North America--Arizona--Folklore.   3. Folklore--Arizona.]   I. Kelly, Laura (Laura C.), ill.
    II. Title. III. Series.
    E99.H7S343   1997
    398.2'089'974--dc20
    [E]
                                                                        96-33280

This edition first published in 1997 by
Gareth Stevens Publishing
1555 North RiverCenter Drive, Suite 201
Milwaukee, Wisconsin 53212 USA

© 1992 by Byron Preiss Visual Publications, Inc. Text © 1992 by Bank Street College of Education. Illustrations © 1992 by Laura Kelly and Byron Preiss Visual Publications, Inc.

Published by arrangement with Bantam Doubleday Dell Books for Young Readers, a division of Bantam Doubleday Dell Publishing Group, Inc., New York, New York. All rights reserved.

BANK STREET READY TO READ™ is a trademark of Bantam Doubleday Dell Books For Young Readers, a division of Bantam Doubleday Dell Publishing Group, Inc.

Printed in Mexico

1 2 3 4 5 6 7 8 9 01 00 99 98 97

The Warrior Maiden

A Hopi Legend

by Ellen Schecter
Illustrated by Laura Kelly

A Byron Preiss Book

Gareth Stevens Publishing
MILWAUKEE

Listen!
Listen to the story of Huh-áy-ay,
the brave Warrior Maiden
who saved her people from death.

Chapter 1
Shadows in the Distance

The sun rises hot and red
over the Hopi pueblo.
Huh-áy-ay runs to the window
and helps her father
lower a ladder.
He is already searching
the desert for danger.

"Be careful," Father warns her.
"Watch for Apache raiders.
Protect the corn.
Protect our people.
Pull up the ladders till we return."

The men and boys
climb down the ladders
and walk into the morning.

Huh-áy-ay and her sisters
help Mother shuck corn.
As they work,
Mother talks about the ways of the Hopi.
"We are peaceful people.
Even our name means peace.
We would rather farm than fight.

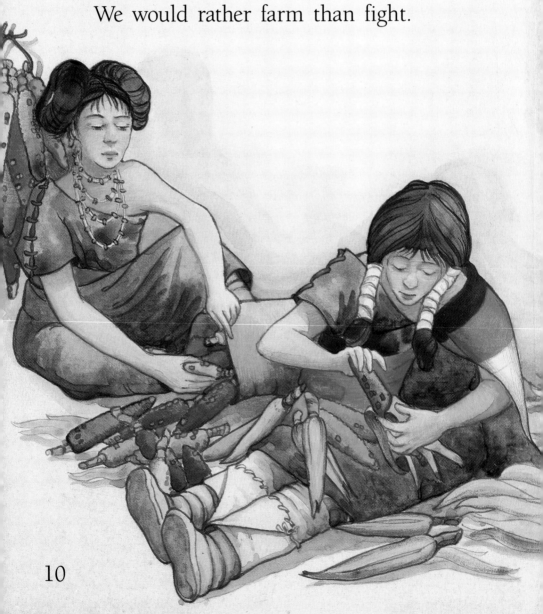

"But we live in a harsh, dry land.
Food is scarce.
The Apache want our corn.
If they attack,
we must be brave and strong.
And if we must fight,
we must fight to win."

The men and boys walk miles and miles
across the desert.
They walk toward a bright green cloud
at the edge of the sky.
The bright green cloud is
the growing crops:
corn, beans, cotton, squash.

The boys kick small stones
down the mesa
to remind the gods to send rain.
The men use long sticks
to plant and weed.
It is hard work.

The small boys flap their arms
and make loud sounds
to scare the birds away.

No one sees the shadows of the raiders
creeping toward the pueblo.

Chapter 2
Watching and Working

Huh-áy-ay keeps watch
as Mother grinds corn.
Elder Sister mixes it with water.
Younger Sister helps.

Huh-áy-ay builds the fire
so she can make bread.
Every day she tries to bake
without burning her fingers.
Ouch!
She burns them again
on the red-hot stone.

Huh-áy-ay sits to rest
but keeps watch the whole time.
The baking bread
smells sweet and good.

Mother washes Huh-áy-ay's hair
in cactus suds.
It is shiny and black
as a crow's wing.
Mother curls one side
in a butterfly shape
and pins it in place.

19

But before Mother can pin up the rest,
Huh-áy-ay sees a shadow.
It moves!

She sees another shadow.
And another.
She hears a strange bird call.
Is it a bird?
Or a man?

Huh-áy-ay peers across the desert.
She sees a flash of red.

She remembers her father's words:
"Be careful. Watch for Apache raiders.
Protect the corn.
Protect our people."

Huh-áy-ay's heart beats like a drum.
"Five, ten, fifteen . . ."
Huh-áy-ay tries to count the shadows,
but there are too many.

"Look, Mother," she whispers.
"Apache! The raiders are coming!"

Mother scoops up the baby
and holds him close.
Younger Sister hides in Mother's skirt,
afraid to blink.

They huddle in the house,
afraid to breathe.
The bird that is not a real bird
screams again.

Huh-áy-ay runs and warns the others:
the other mothers, the girls,
and the men too old
to farm or fight.

"What shall we do?" asks Elder Sister.
"Let's run away," cries Younger Sister.
"We must hide," warns Mother,
"or they will kill us
and take our food."

"Hush! Be quiet! Hide!"
everyone cries.
But the Apache shadows creep closer.
Hiding will not help.
Someone must think of a plan.

Chapter 3
The Warrior Maiden

Huh-áy-ay stands still and thinks.
Her heart gallops like a frightened pony,
but she does not feel helpless.
She has a plan.

"Guard the ladders," she commands.
"Stay out of sight,
but make a lot of noise.
Get drums and beat them.
Get rattles and shake them.
Make them think our pueblo
is full of warriors.
It will give me time to run for help."

Huh-áy-ay is so strong, so sure,
that they all take heart.
Everyone does something.
Some tend the babies.
Some hide the corn.
The rest make the songs
and sounds of war.

Huh-áy-ay slips along the cliff,
hiding in the deep blue shade.
It covers her like the night.

The Apache creep closer.
They hear the banging and rattling.
They hear the songs and sounds of war.
They stop short.
They crouch and hide.
"Maybe they think the pueblo
is full of warriors,"
Huh-áy-ay says to herself.
While their eyes search the pueblo,
Huh-áy-ay slips past.

Her feet pound softly
against the hot ground.
Her hair flies like a black crow's wing.
Her heart pounds louder than drums.
Her breath burns in her chest.

But Huh-áy-ay does not look back.
She runs swift and strong.
She feels her feet against the ground
and her head against the sky.

Huh-áy-ay runs and runs.
The green cloud of corn
is still far away.
Her father and brothers look tiny,
like little dolls.

Huh-áy-ay runs harder.
Now she can see the men planting corn.
Now she sees her youngest brother
flapping his arms to scare the crows.
Now she sees the weapons,
ready on the ground.

Huh-áy-ay calls out her warning.
"Come quickly! Hurry!
Apache raiders are attacking our pueblo.
We are trying to scare them away.
Hurry!"

Huh-áy-ay's father picks up his weapons.
He nods proudly at his daughter.
Huh-áy-ay runs with the men and boys
back through the desert,
back to the pueblo,
under the blood-red sun.

They are just in time.
The raiders are
climbing on one another's shoulders,
climbing the cliffs,
climbing the walls.
Then they see Huh-áy-ay with
the men and boys.

The raiders see weapons flash red in the sun.
They are frightened.
They know they are outnumbered.
They turn and run.
The People are safe.

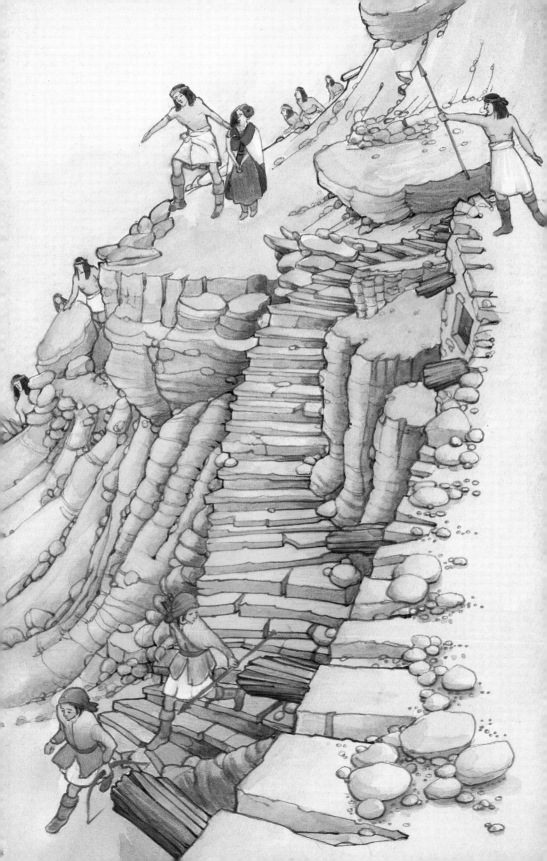

Chapter 4
Peaceful Again

To this day, the Hopi walk in peace.
The men weave cloth;
the women weave baskets.
Men and boys plant and pick corn,
the bread of life.

And each year they celebrate the harvest.
Each person gets an ear of corn.
Each child gets a gift.
And they all sing and dance
in praise of Huh-áy-ay—
the brave and clever Warrior Maiden.

With grateful acknowledgment
to Dr. Frederick Dockstader, former Director
of the Museum of the American Indian,
who told me this story himself.

—E.L.S.